WORKBOOK

FOR

THE GLUCOSE GODDESS

METHOD

The 4-Week Guide to Cutting Cravings, Getting Your
Energy Back, and Feeling Amazing

(A Guide to Jessie Inchauspe's Book)

By Wing Prints

INTRODUCTION

We all want to be healthy, maintain a certain weight, and still be able to eat whatever we want. Most people think this isn't possible; to be healthy, you have to follow a certain diet, cut out certain foods, exercise regularly, etc. What if that doesn't have to be the case? What if you could eat anything you wanted and still be healthy? That is what this book is about. This book is going to teach you 4 hacks that can help you reduce glucose spikes, which cause a lot of issues for the human body and health. The good part is that you'll still be able to eat whatever you want; you may just have to incorporate them in different ways. There are also lots of recipes to help you follow through with these hacks. Who knows? Maybe at the end of the 4 weeks, you'll see the benefits that come with these hacks and decide to stick with them permanently.

THE 2,700 PERSON PILOT EXPERIMENT

The experiment involved 2,700 people between the age of 20-70 from 110 countries. During the experiment, many women got their periods back, some got pregnant, diabetes numbers got better amongst other improvements. The Glucose Goddess method is not a diet because losing weight is not the goal. It is different from a diet because it encourages you to eat more and you don't have to track calories. The Glucose Goddess method is about feeling fantastic in your body size and fixing your body from the inside out. A lot of people are surprised that they lose weight while following this method because they are eating more than usual. This is because when we flatten our glucose curves, our hormones become balanced, our cravings go away and we burn fat more; this is what leads to the weight loss.

IS THE GLUCOSE GODDESS METHOD FOR YOU?

The common belief is that it is only diabetic people that care about their glucose levels. However, scientific progress shows that most people have glucose spikes and this leads to different symptoms and conditions. There are certain questions you need to ask yourself in order to know if this method is for you; some of them include: Do you crave sweet foods? Are you "addicted to sugar"? Do you get tired throughout the day? Do you find it difficult to find the energy to do what you'd like to do? Do you need caffeine to keep you going through the day? Do you experience brain fog? Do you get a "food coma" after eating? Do you need to eat every few hours? Do you feel agitated or angry when you are hungry? Do you feel shaky, light-headed, or dizzy if meals are delayed? Do you have acne? Do you suffer from inflammation? Do you have endometriosis? Do you suffer from dysmenorrhea? Do you experience anxiety and depression? Do you think you can do better than your current state?

If the answer to any of these questions is YES, then the Glucose Goddess Method is for you.

WHAT'S GLUCOSE AGAIN?

Glucose is the fuel source of the body; every cell needs glucose to carry out its specific function. Glucose is very important and the primary method we use to give our body glucose is through food especially starchy and sweet foods. However, the fact that our body needs glucose to perform a lot of

functions doesn't mean we should eat as much sugar and starch as we can. Too much of glucose has a lot of negative effects on the human body. We experience a glucose spike when we take too much glucose at once. This happens to everyone, not just people with diabetes. These glucose spikes can lead to inflammation, aging, low mood, hormone imbalance and overtime serious illnesses like type 2 diabetes and Alzheimer's. These conditions and symptoms are less likely to happen if we flatten our glucose spikes and that is where the hacks in this book come into play.

FIRST, A BIT OF IMPORTANT SCIENCE...

What happens in the body when you experience a glucose spike? First, the mitochondria become overwhelmed because they more glucose than they can handle is coming their way. This causes them to shut down leading to inflammation which reduces their ability to make energy properly which causes us to feel chronic fatigue. Secondly, they accelerate glycation which is responsible for aging. So the more glucose spikes we experience, the faster we age and look older. Glycation also increases inflammation. Thirdly, a lot of glucose spikes mean more insulin in the body and although insulin is beneficial, too much of it reduces fat-burning and it can lead to type 2 diabetes.

SYMPTOMS AND CONDITIONS LINKED TO GLUCOSE SPIKES

1. Cravings: During the crash after a glucose spike we tend to crave more glucose. However, if we steady our curves, we keep our cravings at bay.
2. Chronic fatigue: Too much glucose overwhelms the mitochondria and causes them to quit and since the mitochondria makes energy in our cells, this translates into us feeling tired more than usual.
3. Constant hunger: A meal with less glucose will leave you feeling full for a longer period of time compared to eating a meal with more glucose. In the long-term, a lot of glucose spike confuses our hunger hormones leptin and ghrelin. Leptin tells us when we are full while ghrelin tells us when we are hungry. Eating a lot of glucose causes ghrelin to be more active and when we eat more glucose it causes insulin to store the excess glucose as fat which once again increases the action of ghrelin.
4. Mood: Studies show that when our glucose levels are not stable, we get more irritated. This is because glucose spikes affect certain molecules in the brain that affect our mood. Tyrosine is a neurotransmitter that improves our mood and glucose spikes lead to a reduction of this neurotransmitter.
5. Brain fog: Constant glucose spikes for a prolonged time can damage blood vessels and neurons in the brain which can lead to stroke. Glucose spikes can also reduce the speed at which neurons send signals and we feel this as brain fog, memory issues etc.
6. Skin conditions: A lot of skin conditions are caused by inflammation and inflammation is one of the problems of glucose spikes. Eating the right way and reducing our glucose

curves reduces inflammation and this can help resolve certain skin conditions like acne.

THE FOUR HACKS IN THIS METHOD

These are the most important hacks to start with as they will have a huge impact on your glucose levels and health. They are;

1. Add a veggie starter to one meal a day
2. Have a savory breakfast
3. Have one tablespoon of vinegar a day before the meal that will be highest in glucose
4. After you eat, move

THE FOUR-WEEK PROGRAM

You'll start eating savory breakfast in week 1. You'll include vinegar into your life in week 2. The first two hacks will be continued in week 3 along with the addition of veggie starters. Moving after eating will be added as the fourth hack in week 4. There will be recipes to inspire you and make it easier for you to apply the hacks daily. Remember, you can eat and do whatever you want apart from adding these hacks. It is up to you to continue the hacks once the four weeks are over.

WEEK 1: SAVORY BREAKFAST

OBJECTIVES

1. Eating a savory breakfast every day.
2. Recipes for a savory breakfast.
3. Understanding the benefits of a savory breakfast.

A savory breakfast is a meal that is built around protein and fat; the only sweet thing it consists of is whole fruit. The belief that we need to eat something sweet in the morning to give us energy is false. Research shows that eating sweet things as breakfast is pleasurable but it leads to a glucose spike which makes us tired and will cause us to be hungrier later on. Also, first thing in the morning we are in our FASTED STATE and our body is more sensitive to glucose which is why eating something sweet is the worst thing to do. This week you will discover the benefits if a savory breakfast which include more energy, lesser cravings etc.

HOW TO MAKE A SAVORY BREAKFAST

1. They are built around protein: Protein is the foundation of a savory breakfast; they keep you full and steady.
2. They contain fat: Fat is very important; it is not something that should always be avoided.
3. They contain fiber when possible: Eating fiber in the morning usually mean eating vegetables and this can be very hard to do. However, this can be very beneficial. Any vegetable is fine.
4. They don't contain anything sweet, except optional whole fruit: No dried or fruit juices are allowed. You can eat sweet foods the rest of the day, just not for breakfast.
5. They contain optional starch like bread, potatoes, tortilla for flavor.

HOW TO KNOW IF YOU'RE DOING IT RIGHT

Your savory breakfast is okay of it keeps you full for 4 hours. If you get hungry and it hasn't been 4 hours, increase the quantity of your food. You can combine different breakfast options. You also know you're doing it right if you don't have any cravings in the morning.

THE PERFECT 7-MIN EGGS

You only need 4 eggs, salt and pepper to make this savory breakfast. Heat up some water in a small pot. When the water is bubbling, put in the eggs and let it boil for 7 minutes; it should be ready by then. Drain the water and let the eggs under cold water until they are cool enough to handle. Peel the eggs, cut them in half, put them on a platter, sprinkle salt and pepper on top, and eat them.

SAVORY JAM OR TOAST

For this you need some drained and finely chopped roasted peppers, 7 ounces of crumbled feta, 2 teaspoons of dried oregano (this is optional), toasted sourdough or rye bread, 60ml olive oil, salt and pepper. Preheat the oven to 400°F. Put the chopped red peppers, crumbled feta, oregano and olive oil in a baking dish and mix together well. Put the dish in the oven and bake the mixture for 10 minutes until the pepper and feta have heated through. Remove the dish from the oven and mix again before putting the mixture on the toasted sourdough or rye bread. You can store the remaining mixture to use later.

MY TWO-EGG OMELET

You need a knob of butter, 2 beaten eggs, 20g of crumbled feta, 3 halved cherry tomatoes, salt and pepper. Put a nonstick frying pan on low heat and add butter. Season the beaten eggs with salt and pepper, stir and spread them in a thin layer in the pan so it covers the bottom of the pan. Put the crumbled feta and halved tomatoes on one half of the omelet and let it cook for at least 1½ minutes. Fold the other half of the omelet on the half with toppings, put in a plate and enjoy.

HAPPY HALLOUMI

This recipe is full of protein, fat and fiber. You'll need 2½ ounces of halloumi cut into 2 equal slices, 1 peeled and chopped garlic clove, 1-inch peeled and chopped ginger, 1 teaspoon of curry powder, ¼ teaspoon chili powder, 7 ounces of baby spinach leaves, olive oil, salt and pepper. Heat a small amount of olive oil on medium heat and fry the sliced halloumi for a minute on each side until it is golden all over. Lower the heat and add more olive oil to the empty side of the pan. Add chopped ginger and garlic and fry till they start to crisp. Reduce the heat and add curry and chili powder. Mix with a spatula. Stir the spinach into the garlic and spice mixture and cook till the spinach starts to wilt. Serve on a plate with the halloumi on top then add salt and pepper to taste.

CALIFORNIA QUESADILA

You'll need a knob of butter, 1 small skinless and boneless salmon fillet, 1 6-inch flour or corn tortilla, 1 tablespoon of full-fat cream cheese, ½ pitted and thinly sliced avocado, a drizzle of hot sauce, salt and pepper. Melt the butter on medium heat and once it's bubbling, add the chopped salmon and cook for like 3 minutes (remember to stir from time to time). As the salmon is cooking, put the tortilla on a flat surface and spread the cream cheese on half of it, top with avocado slices and then add the salmon. Drizzle with some hot sauce and season with salt and pepper to your satisfaction. Fold the uncovered half of the tortilla before putting back on medium heat to cook until it is golden and crisp. Transfer to a plate, cut it in half and enjoy.

TODAY I'M FANCY SALMON TOAST

You'll need 1 slice of rye bread, 1 big tablespoon of full-fat cream, 1 slice of smoked salmon cut in half, 2 teaspoons of drained capers and lemon for squeezing. Toast the rye bread, spread the cream cheese on it and top with the salmon and capers. Serve with lemon wedge for squeezing.

AVOCADO TOAST 2.0

Most avocado toasts lack protein which is the main thing needed in a savory breakfast. So to make your avocado toast a savory breakfast, you can add ham, egg, cheese or any other protein you like. You'll need ½ pitted avocado, 1 teaspoon of harissa paste, 1 slice of rye bread, 2 slices of smoked ham, lemon juice (optional), salt and pepper. Mix the avocado flesh and harissa paste together and season with salt and pepper. Toast the rye bread, put the ham slices on it before adding the avocado mixture. Squeeze some lemon juice on it if you want and then eat.

PROSCIUTTO. RICOTTA. FIGS. CHEF'S KISS

You'll need 3 tablespoons of ricotta, 3 slices of prosciutto, a fresh fig cut into 6 wedges, salt, pepper and olive oil. Put the ricotta in a bowl, add a generous amount of salt and pepper, and mix until it is smooth. Top the cheese with prosciutto slices and fig wedges, drizzle everything with olive oil, add some pepper on top and serve.

TOAST PARTY

You'll need 3 slices of dark rye bread, a slice of smoked trout, 2 tablespoons of soft goat cheese, 1 tablespoon of basil pesto, salt and pepper. Toast the slices of bread and top with either the smoked trout or goat cheese or basil pesto. Cut each slice into 2, season with salt and pepper before eating.

AN APPLE WITH SOME CLOTHES ON

Whole fruits can be part of a savory breakfast as long as they come with protein and fat. For this you'll need an apple sliced into rounds, lemon juice, 1½ ounce of sliced cheddar, and a handful of walnut pieces. Dress the apple slices with lemon juice so it won't brown. Put them on a plate, add the cheddar slices, scatter the walnut pieces and then serve.

SAVORY SMOOTHIE

You'll need 2 scoops of protein powder, 1 tablespoon of flaxseed oil, 2 teaspoons of ground flaxseeds, 3½ ounces of frozen fruit, 3 tablespoons of butter. Put all the ingredients in a blender with 100ml of water and blend until it is smooth. Pour into a glass and drink.

BREAKFAST ICE CREAM

You'll need 6 tablespoons of full-fat Greek yoghurt, 1 tablespoon of nut butter, and 50g of frozen mixed berries. Mix the yoghurt and nut butter in a bowl until it is smooth, stir the frozen mixed berries and let the mixture settle for about 2 minutes before eating.

BREAKFAST SALAD

You'll need 4½ ounces of rind trimmed watermelon, 8 trimmed and sliced radishes, 2¼ ounces of crumbled feta, at least 3 roughly chopped mint sprigs, 2 tablespoons of pumpkin seeds, little lime juice and a tablespoon of olive oil. Arrange the ingredients in a bowl, sprinkle with pumpkin seeds and drizzle with lime juice and olive oil.

FIBER-FIRST GARDEN PLATE

You'll need ½ ball of burrata, a small pitted and sliced peach, a small handful of arugulas, 2 tablespoons of chopped pecans, a tablespoon of olive oil, salt and pepper. Arrange the ingredients in a serving bowl, drizzle with olive oil and season with salt and pepper.

LESSONS

1. A savory breakfast is a meal that is built around protein and fat.
2. In our fasted state our body is more sensitive to glucose.
3. Eating sweet things as breakfast is pleasurable but it leads to a glucose spike.
4. Your savory breakfast is okay if it keeps you full for at least 4 hours.

QUESTIONS

1. What does your typical breakfast consist of?

_____

_____

_____

_____

_____

_____

_____

_____

_____

_____

_____

_____

2. How do you feel after you eat something sweet in the morning?

_____

_____

_____

_____

_____

_____

_____

_____

_____

3. What are the effects of having a sweet breakfast?

_____

_____

_____

_____

_____

_____

_____
_____
_____
_____
_____
_____
_____

4.   What are the characteristics of a savory breakfast?

_____
_____
_____
_____
_____
_____
_____
_____
_____
_____

5.   How has following this hack benefitted you?

_____
_____
_____
_____
_____
_____
_____
_____
_____
_____

_____
_____
_____
_____
_____
_____
_____
_____
_____

6.   What changes can you make to your meals to make
this hack more enjoyable for you?

_____
_____
_____
_____
_____
_____
_____
_____
_____
_____
_____
_____
_____
_____
_____
_____
_____

7.   What issues did you have while doing this hack?

_____
_____
_____
_____

WEEK 2: VINEGAR

OBJECTIVES

1. Understanding the vinegar hack.
2. The benefits of acetic acid.
3. Finding the recipe that works for you.

The goal is to take a tablespoon of vinegar a day. This can be done in different ways and at any time of the day. However, the best time to have vinegar is 10 minutes before eating something sweet or starchy. If you feel less tired or your cravings reduce the more you practice this, it is a good sign.

THE SCIENCE

Vinegar contains acetic acid, and this does a lot of good in the body. It reduces how our digestive enzymes turn sugar and starch into glucose, which leads to less glucose spikes. When acetic acid gets into the bloodstream, it penetrates the muscles and causes them to store up free glucose for our next exercise or activity. A tablespoon of vinegar before a meal can reduce the glucose spike of that particular meal by 30%, which has a lot of long-term benefits if done consistently. Acetic acid not only reduces the amount of insulin in our body, but it also has a huge effect on our DNA. It tells our DNA to reprogram and allow our mitochondrial cells to burn more fat. Over time, this can lead to reduced visceral fat.

HOW TO MAKE YOUR OWN VINEGAR HACK

The only thing you need for this hack is vinegar (it can be any vinegar). You can also use other ingredients with the vinegar. However, avoid using agave, honey, maple syrup, or fruit juice.

HOW TO KNOW IF YOU'RE DOING IT RIGHT

This hack should be enjoyable. If you are uncomfortable with the taste, try diluting your vinegar more or reducing the amount of vinegar you use. It is also important to speak to your doctor before doing this hack; don't do it if they do not approve of it.

THE GG CLASSIC

You'll need a tablespoon of any form of vinegar you enjoy. Mix the vinegar and 1¼ cup of water in a glass. It is better to drink it through a straw to protect the enamel of your teeth. Reduce the quantity of the vinegar if it is too strong for you.

THE LEMON OPTION (FOR THOSE WHO CAN'T STAND VINEGAR)

There are some people who do not like vinegar and that is totally fine; you can use lemon juice as an alternative if this applies to you. You'll need a juice of ½ lemon and some ice cubes. Mix the lemon juice with 1¼ cup of water in a glass and some ice. It is also better to use a straw when drinking this.

THE ICE-CUBE TRAY

This is for people who would prefer not to dirty a spoon every day to measure their vinegar. The only ingredient needed is any vinegar of your choice. Pour a tablespoon of your vinegar into each hollow of an ice-cube tray and freeze. When it is frozen, you can put an ice cube into your drink or water each day instead of making a vinegar drink.

THE EMOTIONAL SUPPORT WATER BOTTLE

You can dilute your vinegar in a flask and carry it around in order to do this hack on the go. All you need to do is mix a tablespoon of vinegar and 2½ cup of water in your flask or water bottle.

THE RESTAURANT VINEGAR DRINK

In case you want to do this hack and you are in a restaurant, all you need to do is ask for some vinegar as most restaurants have it. Put a tablespoon of the vinegar into a glass of water, mix and drink before having your food.

TRY-ME MOJITO SLUSHIE

You'll need 2-3 mint sprigs, 1 tablespoon of vinegar, some ice cubes and soda water. Put the mint leaves, vinegar and ice cubes in a blender and blend until the mixture is like a slushie. Pour it into a glass and add soda water to top up. You can also garnish with more mint sprigs if you want to.

GINGER GIANT

You'll need 1¼ inch of peeled and finely grated ginger, a tablespoon of vinegar, some ice cubes, soda water and a lime slice as a garnish (optional). Mix the grated ginger and vinegar in a glass, fill the glass with ice cubes and top up with soda water.

MOTHER APPLE SPRITZER

You'll need 1 teaspoon of grounded cinnamon, 1 tablespoon of vinegar, some ice cubes, soda water, and some cored and sliced apple. Mix the cinnamon and vinegar, pour the mixture in a glass, add some ice cubes and soda water. Put the apple slices and drink.

NOT-ORANGE-JUICE SPRITZER

You'll need 1-inch peeled and roughly chopped ginger, 2 stemmed mint sprigs, 1 stemmed rosemary sprig, orange zest, ¼ teaspoon of ground turmeric, 1 tablespoon of vinegar, some ice cubes and soda water. Put the ginger, mint, rosemary, orange zest, turmeric and vinegar into a glass and gently mash everything together. Add soda water, put some ice cubes in a fresh glass and strain the spritzer into it. You can add a slice of orange or some mint as garnish before drinking.

CAULIFLOWER AND ZA'ATAR PICKLES

You'll need ¾ cup plus 2 tablespoons of vinegar, 1 1/2 tablespoons of za'atar, a small cauliflower with its stalks removed and broken into smaller pieces and 1 tablespoon of salt. Pour the vinegar into a saucepan, add the za'atar and salt and put on medium heat. Allow the liquid to boil before removing from heat. Put the cauliflower florets into a sterilized jar and the hot liquid into the jar. Cover the jar and let its contents cool. You can eat the pickle immediately if you want. However, the liquid will get stronger over time; it can last for about 4 weeks.

THE HOT CINNAMON TEA

You'll need 1 teaspoon of vinegar, ½ teaspoon of ground cinnamon, almost boiling hot water and a cinnamon stick as garnish. Mix the vinegar and cinnamon together in a mug, pour hot water, stir and garnish before drinking.

TURMERIC AND PEPPER TEA

You'll need 1 tablespoon of vinegar, ½ teaspoon of ground turmeric, ½ teaspoon of ground black pepper and almost hot boiling water. Put the vinegar, turmeric and black pepper in a mug, mix together before adding the hot water.

PERFECT PARMESAN DRESSING

You'll need 2 tablespoons of vinegar, 30g of finely grated parmesan, 12 roughly torn basil leaves, 6 tablespoons of olive oil, salt and pepper. Put the vinegar, grated parmesan, basil leaves and olive oil in a bowl and season with salt and pepper. Blend the mixture in a blender until it is smooth and green. You can keep it for 2-3 days but it is better to use immediately.

HOT SRIRACHA DRESSING

You'll need 2 tablespoons of sesame oil, 2 tablespoons of vinegar, 2 tablespoons of sriracha, 2 tablespoons of soy sauce, 4 tablespoons of English mustard and pepper. Put all the ingredients in a jar, seal and shake until it is emulsified. Put in the fridge until you need it.

GREEN GODDESS DRESSING-DIP

You'll need ½ pitted avocado, a small bunch of cilantro, lime juice, 1 tablespoon of Dijon mustard, 2 tablespoons of vinegar, 2 tablespoons of olive oil, salt and pepper. Put all the ingredients in a food processor and blend until it's smooth. It is better to use the dressing immediately but you can also keep it for 24 hours if it is covered and refrigerated.

LESSONS

1. Acetic acid reduces the rate at which our digestive enzymes change sugar and starch to glucose.
2. The best time to have vinegar is 10 minutes before eating something sweet or starchy.
3. You can have your vinegar anyhow you like.
4. Acetic acid reduces the amount of insulin in our body.

QUESTIONS

1. What changes did you notice while doing this hack?

    _____
    _____
    _____
    _____
    _____
    _____
    _____
    _____
    _____
    _____
    _____
    _____
    _____

2.   How has this hack benefitted you?

    _____
    _____
    _____
    _____
    _____
    _____
    _____
    _____
    _____
    _____
    _____
    _____

3.   What issues did you face while doing this hack?

    _____
    _____
    _____

_____
_____
_____
_____
_____
_____
_____
_____
_____
_____
_____
_____

4.   What are the benefits of acetic acid?

_____
_____
_____
_____
_____
_____
_____
_____
_____
_____
_____

5.   What changes can you make to make this hack more enjoyable for you?

_____
_____
_____

WEEK 3: VEGGIE STARTER

OBJECTIVES

1. Understanding the veggie hack.
2. The importance of fiber.

This hack is all about adding fiber to our meals. Fiber is mostly found in vegetables, so the best way to add fiber to your meal is to add some vegetables as a starter. This veggie starter should make up about 30% of your meal. This doesn't mean you have to change how you eat. Another way to achieve this hack is to mix it with the vinegar hack.

THE SCIENCE

Fiber has a very big impact on our glucose levels. When fiber gets to our upper intestines, it forms a protective mesh that can stay in a particular place for hours. This mesh reduces the speed at which glucose enters our bloodstream, thereby reducing our glucose spikes.

HOW TO MAKE YOUR OWN VEGGIE STARTER

Your veggie starter can be simple or fancy; it all depends on how you want it. All you have to do is pick your favorite vegetable, make it however you prefer (it could be raw, cooked, etc.), dress it with some fats or proteins but avoid adding sugar, and then eat it with whatever meal you choose to have at that particular moment. If you're eating in a restaurant, ask for some side salad before you have your main meal, or you can add it as a side to your meal. If you're traveling, you can take some vegetables like baby carrots, cherry tomatoes, or even sliced cucumbers; these don't have to be cooked before they can be eaten.

HOW TO KNOW IF YOU'RE DOING IT RIGHT

You're doing it the right way if veggie starters make up to 30% of each meal you have. Sometimes this might mean you'll eat smaller quantities of your main meal, but remember that eating less is not the goal.

EXPRESS FIBER

You'll need 5 cherry tomatoes, 5 baby carrots, 5 cucumber slices, and 3 big tablespoons of hummus. Put the vegetables listed above or any other vegetable together, then add some hummus in a dipping bowl and eat together.

CAULIFLOWER SALAD

You'll need ½small,l roughly chopped cauliflower, 2 teaspoons of Dijon mustard, 1 tablespoon of apple cider vinegar, 20g of crumbled cheddar, a handful of flat-leaf parsley, 4 tablespoons of olive oil, salt and pepper. Preheat the oven to 425°F, put the chopped cauliflower, 2 tablespoons of the olive oil, salt and pepper in a roasting pan and then put it in the oven. Allow the cauliflower to roast for 25 minutes. You'll then make a dressing by mixing 2 tablespoons of olive oil with the Dijon mustard and apple cider vinegar, some salt and pepper. When the cauliflower is cooked, remove it from the oven, add the cheddar and parsley all over it, drizzle with the dressing and eat.

MY COUSIN'S MISO SPINACH

You'll need 2 teaspoons of tahini, 1 teaspoon of white or brown miso, 1 teaspoon of soy sauce, lemon juice, 75g of spinach, salt and pepper. Mix the tahini, miso, soy sauce and lemon juice with 2 teaspoons of water in a bowl until it is smooth and creamy. Put the spinach all over the mixture and season with salt and pepper.

BEAUTIFUL BATCH OF ROASTED VEGGIES

You'll need a small eggplant cut into smaller pieces, 1 red bell pepper that will also be cut into smaller pieces, 1 small peeled and roughly sliced onion, 1 small zucchini (sliced), 1 tablespoon of basil pesto, a handful of nuts, 2 tablespoons of olive oil, salt and pepper. Preheat the oven to 425°F. on a roasting pan lined with parchment paper, spread all the vegetables, drizzle with olive oil, season with salt and pepper before putting them in the oven to roast for 20-25 minutes. When it is ready, pour into a serving bowl, add the basil pesto, stir and top with nuts. This veggie starter can last for 3-4 days if it is stored in an airtight container and put in the refrigerator.

THE GUMBALL MACHINE

You'll need 7 cherry tomatoes, 7 mini balls of mozzarella, ½ avocado that has been pitted and cut into smaller pieces, 1 tablespoon of balsamic vinegar, 1 tablespoon of olive oil, salt, and pepper. Arrange the tomatoes, mozzarella balls, and avocado slices in a bowl. Drizzle the balsamic vinegar and olive oil, and season with salt and pepper before eating.

BITTER LEAF SALAD WITH YOGHURT DRESSING

You'll need a tablespoon of full-fat Greek Yogurt, lemon juice, 2 tablespoons of finely grated parmesan, 2 handfuls of mixed lettuce leaves, a handful of blanched hazelnuts, 1 tablespoon of olive oil, salt and pepper. Mix the yogurt, lemon juice, parmesan, and olive oil in a bowl to make a dressing and season with salt and pepper. Put the lettuce leaves on a plate and drizzle the dressing on it. Stir for a bit, sprinkle some hazelnuts if you want and serve.

FRENCHIE ASPARAGUS

You'll need 2 teaspoons of Dijon mustard, 1 tablespoon of vinegar, 1 jar of white asparagus, 2 teaspoons of olive oil, salt and pepper. Whisk the mustard, vinegar and olive oil until it makes a dressing and then season with salt and pepper. Put the white asparagus on a plate, put some dressing over it and the season with salt and pepper to your preferred taste.

BACKWARD BROCCOLI

You'll need ¼ head of finely chopped broccoli, 3 tablespoons of full-fat Greek yoghurt, 1½ teaspoon of harissa paste, salt and pepper. Put the broccoli in a heatproof bowl and cover with boiling water for 2 minutes to soften it. Spread the yoghurt on a plate and mix in the harissa. Drain the broccoli and then put it over the yoghurt, season with salt and pepper before serving.

FRIDGE RATATOUILLE

You'll need 1 roughly chopped red onion, 1 eggplant cut into small chunks, 3 garlic cloves, 3 roughly chopped bell peppers, 400g of chopped tomatoes, 2 tablespoons of olive oil, salt and pepper. Heat the olive oil on medium heat, add the chopped onion and eggplant and fry for 2 minutes, add the chopped garlic and fry for 30 seconds. Add the chunks of bell pepper, chopped tomatoes and balsamic vinegar. Stir and cook on high heat for 15 minutes until the vegetables are soft. Season with salt and pepper and allow to cool before serving. This starter can last for 5 days if it is stored well in the refrigerator.

FANCY ZUCCHINI ROLLS TO SHARE

You'll need 60g of ricotta, 2 tablespoons of finely grated parmesan, 50g of spinach, 1 teaspoon of grounded nutmeg, 1 tablespoon of toasted pine nuts, 1 small zucchini (sliced long), salt and pepper. Mix the ricotta, parmesan, spinach, nutmeg and toasted pine nuts in a bowl to make the filling, season with salt and pepper. On the long slices of zucchini spread some of the filling and roll into a spiral. Arrange on a plate and eat.

MY AUNT'S PURPLE RED CABBAGE SALAD

You'll need ¼ of finely sliced red cabbage, lemon juice, 2 tablespoons of pomegranate seeds, 5-6 cilantro sprigs (roughly chopped), 1 tablespoon of olive oil, salt and pepper. Put all the ingredients in a bowl and stir, season with salt and pepper then serve and eat.

BABY RADISHES WITH DILL AND YOGHURT

You'll need 12 halved radishes, 1 tablespoon of full-fat Greek yoghurt, 5-6 finely chopped dill sprigs, 1 tablespoon of olive oil, salt and pepper. Mix the halved radishes, Greek yoghurt, chopped dill and olive oil in a bowl. Season with salt and pepper and then eat.

5-MIN SOUP

You'll need 50g of frozen spinach, 100g of finely chopped broccoli, 1¼ cup of water, 1 tablespoon of white or brown miso, 1 tablespoon of soy sauce and lime juice. Put the frozen spinach and chopped broccoli in a pan with boiling water, place on high heat and allow the vegetables to cook. Stir in the miso, soy sauce and lime juice. Serve and eat.

LAZY TZATZIKI

You'll need half of a large cucumber cut into long pieces, 2 tablespoons of full-fat Greek yoghurt, a handful of stemmed mint, 1 tablespoon of olive oil, salt and pepper. Put all the ingredients in a bowl and mix, season with salt and pepper before serving.

PARMESAN AND BALSAMIC COUPLE

You'll need a big handful of arugulas, 1 tablespoon of balsamic vinegar, 2 tablespoons of shaved parmesan, 2 teaspoons of olive oil, salt and pepper. Mix the arugula, balsamic vinegar and olive oil in a bowl. Season with salt and pepper. Put some shaved parmesan on top and eat.

LOVER'S SALAD

You'll need a handful of salad leaves, 6 halved cherry tomatoes, 6 cucumber slices, 5 stemmed dill sprigs, 15g of crumbled feta, 1 teaspoon of za'atar, lemon juice, 1 tablespoon of olive oil, salt and pepper. Arrange the vegetables on a plate, put some za'atar over them, put some lemon juice and olive oil, season with salt and pepper.

TALENTED TOMATOES

You'll need 15 halved tomatoes, 1 tablespoon of full-fat Greek yoghurt, 1 teaspoon of dried oregano, and 1 tablespoon of olive oil, salt and pepper. Mix the halved tomatoes, yoghurt, oregano and olive oil together, season with salt and pepper to your taste, and serve.

REMEBERED HERB SALAD

You'll need a handful of mixed lettuce leaves, lemon juice, 1 tablespoon of olive oil, salt, pepper and 6-7 sprigs of cilantro, mint and parsley. Mix all the leaves and herbs, drizzle with lemon juice, dress with olive oil and season to your taste with salt and pepper.

BEAUTIFUL BEETS

You'll need 3-4 cooked and sliced small baby beets, a handful of finely chopped dills, a handful of roughly chopped hazelnuts, and 1 tablespoon of olive oil, salt and pepper. Mix the beets, chopped dill and olive oil together, season with salt and pepper to your taste and serve.

LESSONS

1. The best way to add fiber to your meal is to add some vegetables as a starter or a side.
2. Fiber should make up at least 30% of your meals.
3. You don't have to change how you eat to follow this hack.

QUESTIONS

1. What are the benefits of fiber?

_____
_____
_____
_____
_____
_____
_____
_____
_____
_____
_____
_____
_____
_____
_____
_____
_____

2. What changes have you noticed since you started incorporating this hack?

_____
_____
_____
_____
_____
_____
_____
_____
_____
_____
_____
_____
_____
_____
_____
_____
_____
_____

3.	How do you prefer to eat and incorporated vegetables into your meals?

_____
_____
_____
_____
_____
_____
_____
_____
_____
_____
_____

_____
_____
_____
_____
_____
_____
_____

4.　　What issues did you have when practicing this hack?

_____
_____
_____
_____
_____
_____
_____
_____
_____
_____
_____
_____
_____

5.　　How do you feel after following this hack for an extended period of time?

_____
_____
_____
_____
_____
_____

WEEK 4: MOVEMENT

OBJECTIVES

1. Incorporating movement.
2. Dealing with cravings.

Hopefully by this time, the other hacks are becoming a habit and you're seeing the benefits of these hacks. This last hack will have huge benefits for your muscles. Basically, after one of your meals for the day, use your muscles for at least 10 minutes and this should be done within 90 minutes after you finish eating. The movement could be done in different forms like walking, dancing, some light exercises etc. There are a lot of ways to move when doing this hack. You also don't have to start by doing this hack for 10 minutes in the beginning; if 10 minutes feels too much, start slow and work your way up.

THE SCIENCE

Our cells need glucose for energy but the problem is we tend to eat foods that give us too much glucose at once causing a glucose spike which leads to a lot of problems and conditions. However, if you move after eating, this excess glucose is used up by the cells in your muscles thereby reducing your glucose spike. And as a bonus, when we move after eating we reduce our glucose without increasing our insulin levels because the muscles do not need insulin when they are contracting or in use. This benefits us because reduced insulin levels improve our health and can prevent conditions like diabetes. Another good thing is you don't need to change your diet for this hack; eat what you want but make sure you engage in some movement.

HOW TO KNOW IF YOU'RE DOING IT RIGHT

You're doing it right if you find a form of movement that is perfect for you and doesn't seem like too much work. Another way to know you're doing it right is if you feel good after doing some movement. Don't do heavy exercises; let it be some light movement.

LIST OF IDEAS TO COMPLETE THE MOVEMENT HACK

1. Stretch
2. Walk while doing other activities
3. Dance; it could be a 10-minute YouTube dance video or put on your three favorite songs and dance on your own
4. Do some chores
5. Run errands
6. Do some light exercises like calf raises
7. Pilates
8. Hikes
9. Play with your kids or little children around if you can
10. Bike
11. Yoga etc

SOS: CRAVINGS

Although your cravings will reduce as you flatten your glucose curve, it is normal to still have some cravings. This is how you deal with cravings when they come:

Give cravings a 20-minute cooling period: Normally a reduction in our glucose spike should be a signal to eat but because we tend to eat a lot of sweet things, it now happens because the last thing we ate increased our glucose levels drastically. This causes our brain to tell us to eat more sweet things even though we are not hungry. So the next time you have a craving, wait for 20 minutes. If your craving happened because of a reduction of your glucose spike and not actual hunger, it'll be gone in 20 minutes. If it's still there after 20 minutes, you can add some of the other hacks to make it a more beneficial meal.

WEEK 4 IS DONE- NOW WHAT?

Now that you have practiced all the hacks and seen how they affect you, you can decide whether or not you want to stick with them. You can also make some tweaks or little changes to help them work better for you depending on your taste, body system and condition.

LESSONS

1. Having cravings are normal; it's not something that can completely be eradicated.
2. When we move after eating, we reduce our glucose without increasing our insulin levels.
3. Use your muscles for at least 10 minutes a day and this should be done within 90 minutes after you finished eating one of your meals.
4. Practice other hacks with your cravings to make it a more beneficial meal.

QUESTIONS

1. What form of movement have you incorporated into your life?

_____

_____

_____

_____

_____

_____

_____

_____

_____

2. What are the benefits of movement?

_____
_____
_____
_____
_____
_____
_____
_____
_____
_____
_____
_____
_____
_____
_____
_____

3. Why do we have cravings?

_____
_____
_____
_____
_____
_____
_____
_____
_____
_____
_____

_____
_____
_____
_____

4.　　　What are your usual cravings?

_____
_____
_____
_____
_____
_____
_____
_____
_____
_____
_____
_____
_____
_____
_____

5.　　　How do you deal with cravings?

_____
_____
_____
_____
_____
_____
_____

_____

_____

_____

_____

_____

_____

_____

_____

_____

_____

6.   What benefits or changes have you noticed from practicing this hack?

_____

_____

_____

_____

_____

_____

_____

_____

_____

_____

_____

7.   What forms of movement do you enjoy doing the most?

_____

_____

_____

_____

_____

Made in the USA
Coppell, TX
24 October 2024

39133568R00025